Super Science

The Human Body

Richard Robinson

QED Publishing

QED

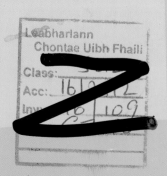

Copyright © QED Publishing 2007

First published in the UK in 2007 by
QED Publishing
A Quarto Group company
226 City Road
London EC1V 2TT
www.qed-publishing.co.uk

A catalogue record for this book is available from the British Library.

ISBN 978 1 84538 914 7

Written by Richard Robinson   Publisher Steve Evans
Edited by Anna Claybourne   Creative Director Zeta Davies
Designed by Balley Design Ltd   Senior Editor Hannah Ray
Consultant Terry Jennings

Printed and bound in China

Picture credits
Key: T = top, B = bottom, C = centre, L = left, R = right, FC = front cover

Corbis: p9 br Matthias Kulka/zefa; p10 Robert Picket; p13 Visuals Unlimited;
p23 Herbert Spichtinger/zefa; p27 Wolfgang Kaehler.
Getty Images: p17 Nancy Honey/Photonica.
HSS Hire/www.hss.com: p7.
Photolibrary Group Ltd: p5 tr.
Science Photo Library: p5 bl & br Steve Gschmeissner; p5 cb CNRI;
p9 ct Prof. S. H. E. Kaufmann & Dr. J. R. Golecki; p18 Eye of Science; p26 Martin Dohrn;

Words in **bold** can be found in
the Glossary on page 31.

Contents

Who are you?

Your body is an amazing machine, made of thousands of different parts. But even more than that, you are a person, different from all other people. You are YOU!

Working together

As well as being yourself, you are part of a great family of humans. You depend on other people. You work with your family, teachers and friends on plans and explorations.

One of the things we humans do a lot is learn about things, and use our discoveries to help us explore further. We have explored all the lands and seas of the Earth. We have even explored the Moon. We might go and explore Mars soon.

We have also explored the human body, and how it works. This book is about what we have discovered.

Above: It is human nature to explore and try to understand how things work.

Left: Humans are social and gregarious, which means we like to be together and to interact. We do many things in teams, because it often works better.

Cells

Your body is built from tiny units called **cells**, just as a house is built from bricks. Most cells contain a headquarters called a **nucleus**. It contains instructions for building and running the whole body, written using a substance called DNA.

Cells come in different shapes and sizes, and do different jobs. For example, skin cells are flat, and join together at the edges. They are being produced constantly, because the outer layer of skin cells is constantly being rubbed off.

Muscle cells make the muscles contract, or get shorter, to make your body move. Bone cells turn themselves solid to become your bones. Red blood cells carry **oxygen** around the body.

Nerve cells are the strangest of all. They form long strands, linking your brain to different parts of your body. They carry messages between the body and the brain.

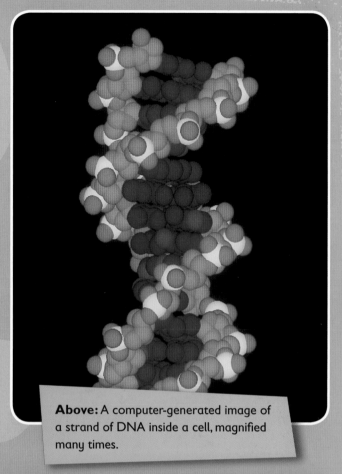

Above: A computer-generated image of a strand of DNA inside a cell, magnified many times.

Different types of cells

Nerve cells

Blood cells

Muscle cells

Food

We eat cake, but we don't turn into cake. How does our food change into us? It's all because of the way our bodies break down food.

Breaking it down

Food is made of billions of tiny **particles**. When you eat something, it is mashed up into juice by your stomach. The juice is then sent to your intestines. The intestines break it down into the tiny bits it is made of. These are then taken to various parts of the body, where they are turned into hair, fingernails, eyes, muscles, bones and all the other parts of you – or used to give your muscles energy to move.

Above: Cake, like all foods, is made up of different substances which can be useful to your body.

The digestive system

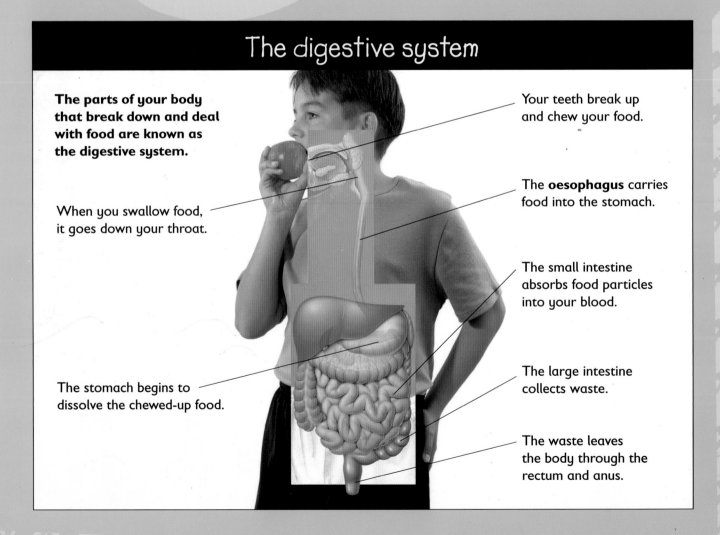

The parts of your body that break down and deal with food are known as the digestive system.

When you swallow food, it goes down your throat.

The stomach begins to dissolve the chewed-up food.

Your teeth break up and chew your food.

The **oesophagus** carries food into the stomach.

The small intestine absorbs food particles into your blood.

The large intestine collects waste.

The waste leaves the body through the rectum and anus.

If the food you eat is not used up by exercise, it can become fat.

How can you find out what is in your food? See page 30.

Food as fuel

A lot of your food doesn't go to build you, but to drive you. It is like fuel in a car; when you exercise you use it up. That's why, after a busy day of running around, you are starving hungry.

If you don't take enough exercise, some of the food you eat is stored around your body as fat. If you want to lose the fat, you need to exercise regularly.

To help you turn food into fuel, your body needs oxygen, which is easy to find. It's in the air. All you have to do is breathe. When you run around you need more oxygen. You get it by panting.

Above: Oxygen is a gas that helps burning. For example, this welder is using a tank of oxygen to help burn fuel to create heat. Exercise makes you hot too, because the oxygen you breathe helps to 'burn' your food and turn it into energy.

Blood

Your blood has several important jobs to do. It transports dissolved food around your body to be used as fuel and to build cells. It removes waste products so that they can be **excreted** in your **urine**. It carries oxygen around, to help your cells burn fuel so that you can move around. Lastly, blood checks all around your body for damage and diseases, and helps to fix them.

Scabbing over

If something cuts your skin, fragments of special blood cells create a web across the gap to stop the blood flowing out. More blood cells get caught in the web, forming a scab.

How can you help your body to deal with cuts? See page 30.

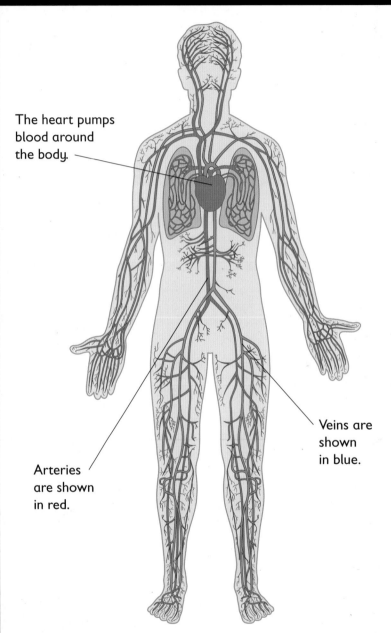

Blood flow around the body

The heart pumps blood around the body.

Arteries are shown in red.

Veins are shown in blue.

Blood flows around your body along blood vessels called veins and arteries. It collects oxygen from your lungs and delivers it to the rest of your body. When blood is carrying lots of oxygen, it is red. When it has delivered its oxygen, it turns a darker, purplish colour.

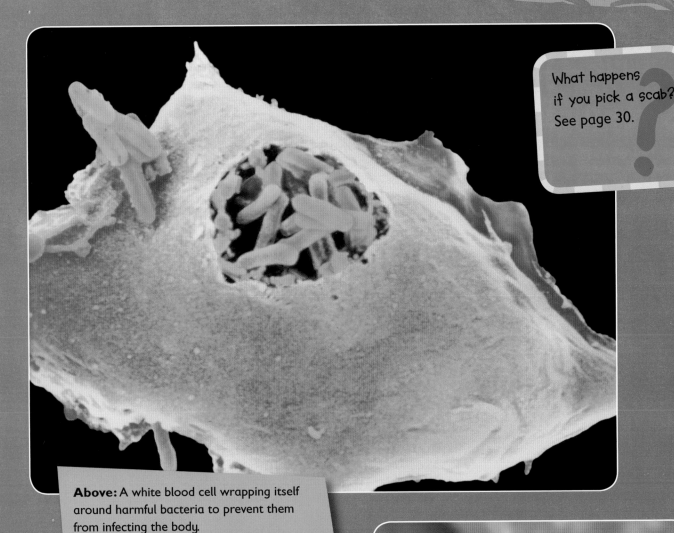

What happens if you pick a scab? See page 30.

Above: A white blood cell wrapping itself around harmful bacteria to prevent them from infecting the body.

Battling germs

If germs get into your body, there are white blood cells in the blood waiting to do battle with them. These are larger than the red blood cells. They attack germs and eat them.

The red area around a cut is where the battle against germs is hottest. Yellow **pus** is the remains of white blood cells and germs that have died in the fight.

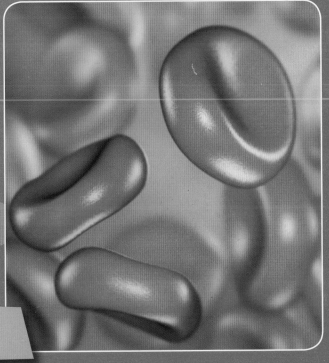

Right: Red blood cells make up around 40% of your blood. They carry oxygen around the body.

Bones

Three-quarters of you is actually water. It doesn't slosh around because it is mixed with other materials in your flesh, like the water in a jelly. Your flesh doesn't wobble like a jelly either, because it is held firm by bones. If all your bones disappeared right now you would flop to the floor in a jelly-like blob.

Animal bones

Different animals have different kinds of skeleton. Snails have a shell which they live in. Insects have an 'exoskeleton' on the outside, like a suit of armour ('exo-' means 'outside'). Worms have no skeleton at all.

But larger animals like us have our bones on the inside. As well as holding us up and helping us move, bones protect our internal **organs**, such as the brain and heart.

Above: We need bones to give our bodies a framework. Without them, we couldn't sit up, walk or talk.

Left: Worms don't have any bones at all. They have jelly-like bodies and move by wriggling along the ground.

Can you think which bones are there to help you do things, and which are purely for protection? See page 30.

Bendy bones

Bones are hard because they contain a chemical called calcium carbonate. Try taking some thin leftover chicken bones and leaving them in a cup of vinegar for a day. They will go bendy! The vinegar dissolves some of the minerals the bones are made of, making them softer. You can tie the bendy bones in knots. Then, if you leave them in the air, they'll go hard again.

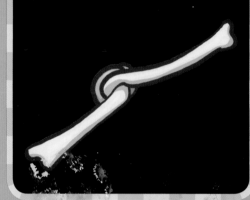

Strong and light

Bones need to be stiff, strong and light. They have ridges, called 'trabeculae' which follow the lines of main stress and strain in the bone, to make it strongest where it needs to be strongest.

When the clever structure of bone was first revealed, in the 1880s, French architect Gustave Eiffel was so impressed that he designed his famous tower to look a little like a thigh bone.

The Skeleton

A human skeleton is made up of 206 separate bones, linked together by moveable joints.

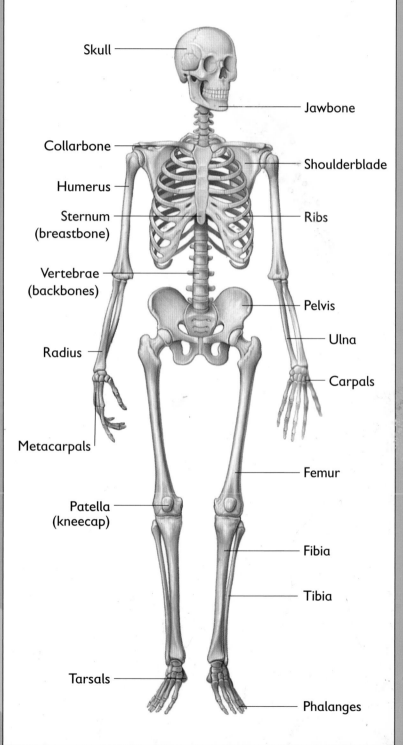

Skull

Jawbone

Collarbone

Shoulderblade

Humerus

Sternum (breastbone)

Ribs

Vertebrae (backbones)

Pelvis

Radius

Ulna

Carpals

Metacarpals

Femur

Patella (kneecap)

Fibia

Tibia

Tarsals

Phalanges

Muscles

The picture opposite shows human muscle seen through a microscope. You can see the fibres it is made up of. To make a muscle work, alternate fibres pull on each other, making the whole muscle contract, or get shorter. Muscles work in pairs to pull on bones to make them move.

Muscles and movement

Some muscles are operating all the time. Your heart beats and your lungs pump continuously, without you thinking about them. (Just as well; there wouldn't be much time for sleep if you had to remind your heart to pump every second!)

Some muscles are situated a long way from the body parts they move. For example, your feet are operated by the calf muscles, behind the shins. They are attached to long strings called **tendons**, which join onto your foot and toe bones. That's why you must rub your calf if you get cramp in your foot.

Muscle make-up

Muscle contains two different types of tiny strands, or filaments, called **actin** and **myosin**. To make a muscle contract, they pull into each other so they overlap. (That also makes the muscle bulge outwards.)

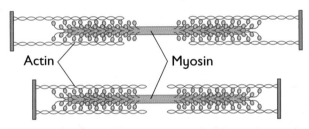

Actin   Myosin

Make a waving hand

YOU WILL NEED:
A pair of scissors
Stiff card
Two drawing pins
Wooden ruler
String

Wiggle the strip to make the hand wave!

First, draw round your own hand onto stiff card. Cut out the hand-shape. Now cut a strip of card, about 2cm across and as long as the hand is wide. Using two drawing pins, fix the hand to one end of a ruler, and the strip of card to the other, as in the picture. Use two pieces of string to make 'tendons' joining them together.

Above: Muscle is made up of millions of tiny fibres, seen here under a microscope.

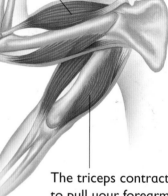

Muscles work in pairs to make your bones move.

The biceps contracts to pull your forearm bone up and bend your elbow

The triceps contracts to pull your forearm bone back down and straighten your elbow.

Muscle and bone

Bones can't make you move by themselves, and nor can muscles. Bones and muscles have to work together, with muscles pulling on bones to move them. Muscles are arranged in pairs. Each pair can pull on a bone to move it one way or the other.

Right: Sports players often injure their muscles and tendons by pulling, twisting or tearing them. Footballers often damage the Achilles tendon, at the back of the ankle.

Can you think of other parts of you that use tendons in the same way? See page 30.

The nervous system

The nervous system is made up of a set of connections, called nerves, that link your brain to the rest of your body. Nerves also carry messages around inside your brain. A nerve is a type of cell. Nerves are very unusual cells because they are so long. Part of the cell is stretched out to a long, thin strand, running from your brain to another body part, such as your leg.

To and fro

When your brain wants you to do something, such as pick up a drink, it sends a message along a nerve to your muscles, telling them to move. Messages can travel the other way, too. As well as carrying messages from your brain, your nerves stand guard over your body. They tell the brain if there is heat, pressure, damage or disease in any region of the body.

Above: The nervous system keeps your body in touch with your brain. It tells the brain what is happening to other parts of your body.

Below: On the road, drivers should keep a good distance away from other cars, because it takes time for the nervous system to react to emergencies and slow down.

Reaction-time testing

YOU WILL NEED:

A 30cm ruler

Pen and paper

To test someone's reaction time, hold a ruler vertically with your hand at the top. Ask the person being tested to hold their hand open around the bottom of the ruler. When you let go, they have to grab the ruler as soon as they can. Don't give any warning of when you are about to let go. If they take more than a quarter of a second to react, they will miss the ruler. If they catch it, you can mark their reaction time by seeing how far down the ruler they are holding it. If you can, test a number of people and compare the results. Who reacts the fastest?

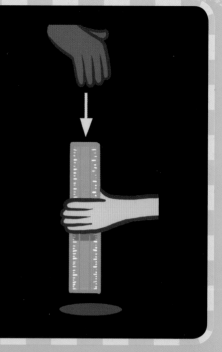

Pain signals

Have you noticed that when you stub your toe, the pain takes some time to arrive? Three different sorts of nerves are involved. The first works quickest, whipping your foot out of danger before you know anything about it. This is called a **reflex**. The second type of nerve sends a quick message to the brain to say that something is badly wrong. Then you have to wait until the third type of nerve can slowly transmit the full damage report. That's when the pain begins.

Can you think of any part of you where there are no nerves? Are there any places which cannot feel heat, pain or pressure? See page 30.

Nerve pathways

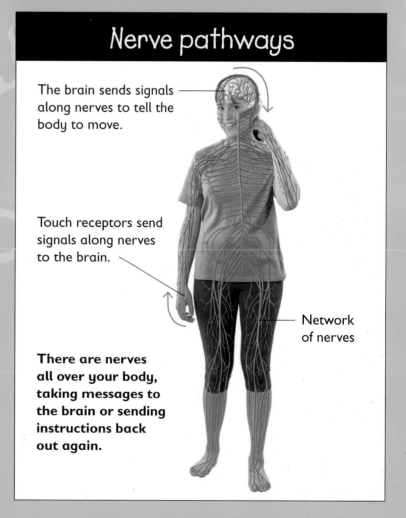

The brain sends signals along nerves to tell the body to move.

Touch receptors send signals along nerves to the brain.

Network of nerves

There are nerves all over your body, taking messages to the brain or sending instructions back out again.

The brain

Your brain is a very busy organ. It has to listen to all the messages coming in from the eyes, ears, nose and other sense organs. Then it has to send messages out to the muscles to do things in response. It also has many other jobs, such as controlling your breathing, balance, thoughts, memories, dreams and emotions.

Memory

The ability to store memories is an important part of the brain's duties. Once you have learned how to ride a bike the memory is kept for ever. If you stop riding for 50 years, then climb on a bike again, the skill is still there. On the other hand, you can sometimes forget a phone number in seconds. Why the difference?

You have two sorts of memory. All memories start life in a part of the brain called the **hippocampus**. But while short-term memories last only for a few seconds, long-term memories are stored all around the brain, and can remain there for years.

Above: You use your memory every day to find things, remember names and faces, speak and do everyday tasks, such as finding your car in the car park.

Parts of the brain

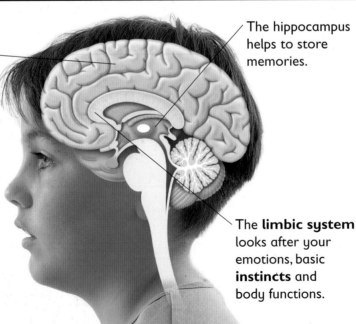

The **cerebrum** thinks, controls your actions and collects signals from your sense organs.

The hippocampus helps to store memories.

The **limbic system** looks after your emotions, basic **instincts** and body functions.

What are your earliest memories? Ask your teacher or parent about theirs.

Brain training

Skills and talents must be practised to make them better. Football practice means training for the brain as well as the body, to judge distances, angles and forces. The brain is also very important in the subtle craft of getting on with your friends and avoiding disagreements with others. You learn to do things like this through the experiences that you go through and remember.

Optical illusions

Your brain sometimes struggles to make sense of the world around you. Optical illusions can trick and confuse the brain. Try looking at this picture. Do you think it shows a duck or a rabbit? You may be able to see both, but your brain wants to interpret the picture as one or the other. It won't let you see both at once.

Left: Your brain learns by storing things in its memory. This is how you revise for an exam, learn a new language or remember history dates.

When we talk together, we use our cerebrums to share our thoughts by listening, thinking and speaking.

Sight and hearing

Sight and hearing are two of the five senses: sight, hearing, smell, taste and touch. Many people think of them as the most important senses.

Seeing

Seeing works by sensing light that bounces off objects around you. Light enters the eye and is focused on a layer of cells at the back of the eye, called the retina. When light hits a cell in the retina, a message zooms along a nerve to the brain. The brain pieces together the information, like a jigsaw, to make a picture.

The retina has colour receptors, called **cones**, that can detect green, red and blue light. Other receptors, called **rods**, detect white light.

How the eye works

Lens
The lens focuses the light onto the retina.

Pupil
Light enters the eye through the pupil.

Retina
The image that forms from the retina is upside-down. The brain has to flip it the right way up again.

Optic nerve
Signals travel from the retina to the brain along the optic nerve.

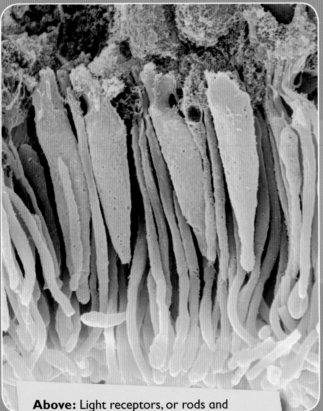

Above: Light receptors, or rods and cones, in the retina of the eye, seen under a microscope.

The blue receptor cells in the retina work slightly better in dim light than the red and green receptors. Can you think how theatre lighting designers and book illustrators use this fact? See page 30.

Below: Your brain is quite brilliant at sifting through different sounds, sorting out one from another. For instance, in a crowded room, you can focus on the voice of the person you're talking to, and ignore the other noises.

Hearing

Your sense of hearing lets you detect sounds. Sound travels through the air as a series of vibrations, which rattle against a delicate piece of skin inside your ear called the **eardrum**. The vibrations are passed deep into your ear, where they are turned into signals that are sent to your brain. The brain examines the signals and works out the sounds.

Batty behaviour

Bats can see with their ears! They send out sounds in high squeaks, then use the echo to work out where they are. Humans can tell a little about the surroundings from echoes, though we can't do it as well as bats. Try shutting your eyes while a friend leads you around. Can you tell when you are near a building, in a corridor or in a wide open space?

Parts of the ear

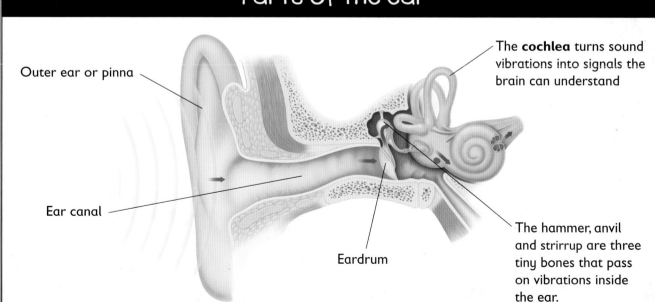

Outer ear or pinna

The **cochlea** turns sound vibrations into signals the brain can understand

Ear canal

The hammer, anvil and stirrup are three tiny bones that pass on vibrations inside the ear.

Eardrum

Taste and smell

Two of the five senses are very similar to each other in a lot of ways. Taste and smell both involve the same area of the body (the nose and tongue are closely linked), and the same area of the brain. Taste and smell might seem like unimportant senses, but they are both vital – your life could depend on them. A bad taste could warn you of poison, and a strange smell could mean danger in the form of smoke or gas.

Smell

Your nose smells by identifying different types of **molecules** as they waft up your nostrils. Smell is particularly useful for knowing what is happening out of sight. If the house next door is on fire, for example, your nose finds out long before your ears or eyes have any idea.

The nose knows

To test your nose's tasting power, try holding your nose when you eat. You won't be able to taste much at all.

Above: When milk has gone off, it's your nose that tells you not to drink it.

The tongue and nose

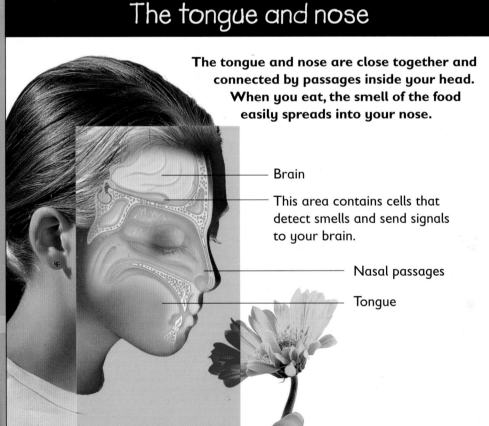

The tongue and nose are close together and connected by passages inside your head. When you eat, the smell of the food easily spreads into your nose.

Brain

This area contains cells that detect smells and send signals to your brain.

Nasal passages

Tongue

Above: Our senses of taste and smell allow us to enjoy some foods, and dislike others. Which is your favourite food here?

Taste

Your tongue can only taste five different flavours, using receptors in the taste buds. They are saltiness, sweetness, bitterness, sourness and a fifth taste called **umami**, meaning savouriness. The reason you can identify thousands more tastes than this is that your nose helps you taste as well, by detecting the food's smell when it is in your mouth.

Did you know?

- An average person can detect 5000 smells.
- Your sense of smell is at its best when you are 10 years old. After that it gets worse and worse.
- A dog's sense of smell is masses better than a human's. Dogs have over 40 times as many smell-detecting cells in their noses as we do.

Touch and proprioception

Your skin is covered with sensors to detect things that touch you. Most of the time you can ignore touch messages, such as the feeling of your clothes on your skin, because they are not that important. But if something unexpected happens – for example, if you have a stone in your shoe – your brain is alerted and you feel it.

Around the body

The number of touch sensors you have in your skin varies in different parts of the body. For example, you often use your hands to touch and feel things, so they have a lot of touch sensors. Your back has far fewer, because it's rarely used for touching things.

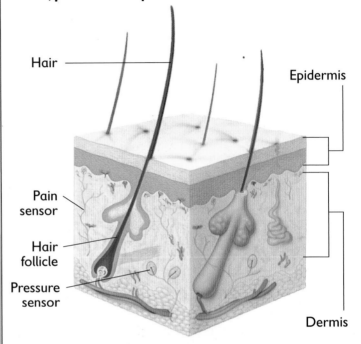

Under your skin

Different touch sensors in your skin detect heat, cold, pressure and pain.

Hair

Epidermis

Pain sensor

Hair follicle

Pressure sensor

Dermis

Touchy-feely

Find out how sensitive your fingers are, compared with your back. (Get someone to help with this.)

YOU WILL NEED:
Two sharp pencils
A ruler

Shut your eyes and ask a friend to tap your finger with two pencil tips held 3cm apart. Can you feel them both? What if the pencils are closer together?

There will come a point when they feel like one tap, not two. Measure the distance and then do the same on your back. What's the difference?

Proprioception

Proprioception (pronounced 'pro-pree-o-sep-shun') is a kind of touch sense that tells you where your body is and what position it is in, thanks to touch sensors in your muscles and tendons. If you ever wake up with a 'dead' arm you'll understand how vital proprioception is. Until the sense returns, it feels as if your arm is not really your own.

Proprioception is essential for doing things like walking, standing upright and dancing. It also lets you touch your nose with your eyes closed. Try it!

Can you imagine life with no sense of touch or proprioception? You would have to think about and plan every move!

Right: A pianist's brain knows exactly where all ten fingers are without thinking about them.

Left: Proprioception tells a footballer exactly where his arms and legs are all the time.

Emotions and instincts

Emotions are controlled by an area in the centre of the brain called the limbic system. This is where fear begins, and anger, and love, happiness and disgust. **Instincts** are automatic reactions and ways of behaving, such as closing your eyes when you sneeze.

Big and small feelings

Some emotions help to keep you alive. Disgust stops you from eating food that smells rotten. Fear keeps you away from cliff edges. Love makes people look after each other.

But even small emotions, such as mild liking, start in the limbic system. Small emotions allow you to make smaller choices. Would you like an apple or a banana? Without a small preference – a tiny emotion – you could spend all day making your mind up.

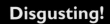

Disgusting!

Disgust is very easy to feel. Talk with your friends about your favourite foods and weird food combinations. You will find that when one of you says something is great (Broccoli? Sprouts? Bacon and marmalade? Ice cream and chips?), others are saying "yuk!" and looking disgusted.

Left, above & above right: We reveal our emotions on our faces, and we can usually read other people's feelings from their faces too. Can you tell what the facial expressions on these pages show?

Automatic reactions

A lot of your behaviour is automatic. When you jerk your head away from foul smells, or when someone blows in your eyes and you blink, you don't stop to think about it. These are called reflexes.

You also have 'instinctive' reactions, which are equally hard to control. The feeling of panic you sometimes feel, with your heart pounding, your hair standing on end, and your eyes staring, is one example. This is the body instinctively preparing you for an emergency.

Sometimes people have different emotions for days of the week. Do you have a favourite day? Or an especially bad day? Do the days have colours or sounds for you? See page 31.

Above: Fear of spiders is an instinct. About 10% of humans are born with it.

Staying the same

As well as dealing with emotions, the limbic system looks after your most basic needs. Have you enough food in your body? Is there enough air for you to breathe? Do you need to start breathing harder because you are exercising? Your body is constantly trying to make sure you have what you need by a process called 'homeostasis' – which means 'staying the same'.

Body checks

Your brain constantly monitors the blood flowing through it. If necessary, it tells organs called glands to release chemicals called hormones into the blood. If you start to run out of air, for instance, a sudden rush of a hormone called adrenaline will cause you to panic and struggle to escape. Other hormones control the amount of sugar in your blood, and the rate at which you grow.

Have you ever experienced claustrophobia in a confined space? See page 31.

Path of hormones

The brain sends signals to your glands to release a hormone called adrenaline.

The adrenaline makes your heart beat faster.

When you are exercising, hormones tell the heart to pump harder.

Above: Goosebumps happen when tiny muscles pull the fine hairs all over your body into an upright position.

Above: Furry mammals, such as these monkeys, often fluff up their fur in the cold, just as humans used to. It keeps them warm by trapping a layer of warm air close to the skin.

Hot and cold

One of the body's jobs is to keep itself at the right temperature. When we are too hot, the limbic system makes us pant, sweat and slow down. When we are cold, we huddle up and shiver to make our muscles warm up.

Our ancestors used to be hairy, and when it was cold, tiny muscles would make the hairs fluff up like a big thick duvet. The hairs are much finer and shorter now, but the same effect still happens, causing goosebumps.

Getting hot makes you look red. The limbic system makes the blood flow close to the skin to help heat escape.

When you're cold, you're more likely to go pale. The limbic system closes down the blood vessels near the skin, to retain heat inside the body.

Babies and growing up

What makes you, you? It's partly to do with the qualities and features you were born with, which you got from your parents, and partly to do with the things you experience as you grow up.

Passing it on

When two parents have a baby, each of them contributes one cell – an egg cell from the mother, and a sperm cell from the father. The cells join together and grow into a baby. This means that you get a mixture of features and abilities from both your parents. Which of your parents are you most like?

But there is also another part of you which is not from your parents; the you that has been learning how to cope with our world.

Above: Through time, more and more generations of people are born, grow up and have their own babies.

How cells make babies

To make a baby, a male sperm cell and a female egg cell join together. This creates a new cell called a **zygote**, which can grow into a new baby.

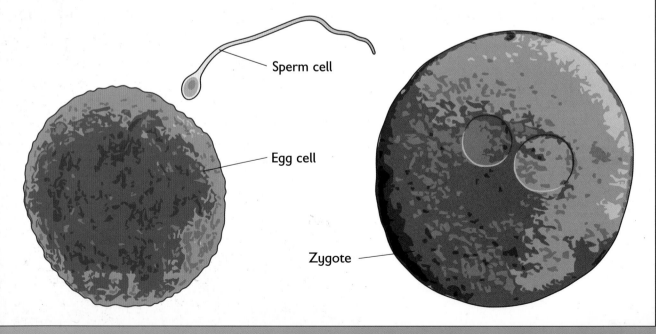

Sperm cell

Egg cell

Zygote

Passed-on features

These are all features that you get from your parents.
See how many people in your class have the following:

1 Freckles

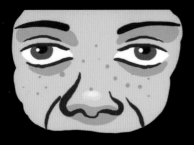

2 Dimpled cheeks

3 Ears with hanging-down earlobes

4 Ability to roll their tongue into a tube

5 Ability to bend their little finger independently of the third finger

Do any two people have the exact same scores?

Learning through experience

You have been on a long journey since you were a baby. To begin with, you were not even in control of your arms and legs. But every day you learned something new – how to reach, eat, walk, talk, tell silly jokes and deal with parents. Now you know lots and you can do plenty of things.

You haven't finished yet. Soon you will make a great leap forward to become an adult. As an adult, you will be able to have babies of your own. Then you will use your body to carry them and look after them, and you will use your brain to love them – and to tell them silly jokes!

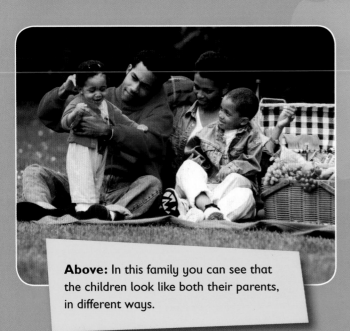

Above: In this family you can see that the children look like both their parents, in different ways.

Questions and answers

How can you find out what is in your food? (page 7)

If you look at the labels on food packaging, you can see what kinds of food you are eating. Does your food contain salt, fat or sugar? (Sucrose, fructose, glucose and honey are all forms of sugar.) What else is in your food?

How can you help your body to deal with cuts? (page 8)

Antiseptic kills germs. If you put it on a cut quickly, you can kill many of the germs before the white blood cells even get there. If the infection remains, medicines can also help to kill the germs.

What happens if you pick a scab? (page 9)

The web that is pulling the skin together gets broken and the skin springs apart. If you keep doing it, the skin stays separated – and then you'll end up with a scar.

Can you think which bones are there to help you do things, and which are purely for protection? (page 10)

The skull looks like a crash helmet, and does the same job. The ribs are a protective cage, although they also help with breathing. The kneecap protects the knee joint. The main back, arm, leg, foot and finger bones help you move around and do things.

Can you think of other parts of you that use tendons the same way? (page 13)

The muscles that operate your fingers are up near your elbow and are connected to your fingers by tendons. Try gripping your arm just below the elbow and wiggling your fingers. You'll feel the muscles moving.

Can you think of any part of you where there are no nerves? Are there any places which cannot feel heat, pain or pressure? (page 15)

Hair, fingernails and parts of your teeth have no nerves.

Blue receptor cells in the retina work slightly better in dim light than red and green receptors. Can you think how theatre lighting designers and book illustrators use this fact? (page 18)

Theatre and film lighting designers use blue light to signify night-time. Book illustrators draw pictures with blue shading to show night scenes.

Sometimes people have different emotions for days of the week. Do you have a favourite day? Or an especially bad day? Do the days have colours or sounds for you? (page 25)

Sometimes people can taste colours, or see music. It's called synesthesia (sin-ess-thees-ia), and is quite common.

Have you ever experienced claustrophobia in a confined space? (page 26)

Claustrophobia is one of a number of fears which many people suffer from – such as fear of heights, unfamiliar surroundings, spiders or dogs. Perhaps you know of some others.

Glossary

Actin – One of the two types of fibre that muscles are made of.

Cells – The basic building block of all living things.

Cerebrum – The outer part of the brain, which thinks, plans actions and makes the muscles carry the actions out.

Cochlea – The organ in the middle ear which turns sound vibrations into nerve signals that the brain can understand.

Cones – Cells in the retina, at the back of the eye, which can detect coloured light.

Eardrum – Part of the ear that collects sound vibrations from the air and passes them inside the ear.

Excrete – to get rid of waste from the body.

Hippocampus – Organ in the brain where memories are held before they either fade or are moved into long-term memory.

Instinct – Behaviour which you are born with, rather than behaviour you learn.

Limbic system – The central area of the brain, which looks after basic needs such as hunger, thirst and temperature.

Molecule – the smallest particle of a substance.

Myosin – One of the two types of fibre that muscles are made of.

Nucleus – The control unit of a cell.

Oesophagus – The tube joining the mouth to the stomach.

Organ – Any part of the body which does a particular job, such as the liver, heart, lungs or brain.

Oxygen – A gas found in the air, which humans need to breathe in to make the body work.

Particle – a very small pice of something.

Pus – A thick yellow liquid found in wounds, made up of dead cells and germs.

Reflex – An automatic reaction, such as blinking when a puff of air hits your eyes.

Rods – Light-sensitive cells in the retina, at the back of the eye.

Tendon – Body part that attaches muscles to bones.

Umami – A savoury taste, one of the basic tastes the tongue can detect.

Urine – Liquid waste that is separated from the blood by the kidneys.

Zygote – The very first cell of a new baby, formed when a sperm joins with an egg.

Index